SNAKES

Published by Creative Education, Inc., 123 South Broad Street, Mankato, Minnesota 56001

Printed by permission of Wildlife Education, Ltd.

ISBN 0-88682-331-5

SNAKES

Created and Written by
John Bonnett Wexo

Zoological Consultant
Charles R. Schroeder, D.V.M.
Director Emeritus
San Diego Zoo &
San Diego Wild Animal Park

Scientific Consultants
James Bacon, Ph.D.
Curator of Reptiles
San Diego Zoo

Richard Ethridge, Ph.D.
Professor of Biology
San Diego State University

Creative Education

Art Credits

Pages Six and Seven: Barbara Hoopes; **Pages Eight and Nine:** Barbara Hoopes; **Page Nine: Bottom,** Drawing by Dick Oden; **Page Ten: Upper Center,** Walter Stuart; **Lower Left,** Walter Stuart; **Page Eleven: Upper Center,** Dick Oden; **Pages Twelve and Thirteen:** Lisa French; **Page Twelve: Upper Right,** Karl Edwards; **Page Fourteen: Center,** Walter Stuart; **Pages Fourteen and Fifteen: Bottom,** Karl Edwards; **Pages Sixteen and Seventeen:** Dick Oden; **Page Seventeen: Center Right,** Drawing by Dick Oden; **Page Eighteen: Lower Left,** Drawings by Karl Edwards; **Upper Right,** Map by Udo Machat; **Pages Eighteen and Nineteen: Bottom,** Geri Nelson and Walter Stuart; **Pages Twenty and Twenty-one:** Dick Oden.

Photographic Credits

Cover: M. P. Kahl *(Bruce Coleman, Inc.)*; **Page Ten: Upper Left,** John Tashian; **Upper Right,** Michael Fogden *(Animals Animals)*; **Center Left,** Elizabeth Burgess *(Ardea);* **Center Right,** Elizabeth Burgess (Ardea; **Page Eleven: Upper Left,** Ron Garrison/Zoological Society of San Diego; **Center Left,** both by K. H. Switak; **Center,** Copyright Peter B. Kaplan 1981; **Center Right,** John Tashjian; **Lower Left,** Zig Leszczynski *(Animals Animals);* **Lower Right,** Anthony Bannister *(Animals Animals);* **Page Thirteen: Upper Right,** Tom McHugh *(Photo Researchers);* **Page Fourteen: Lower Left,** Zig Leszczynski *(Animals Animals);* **Upper Right,** Candice Bayer *(Bruce Coleman);* **Page Fifteen: Upper Right,** C. A. Bank *(Bruce Coleman);* **Middle Right,** all three photographs by Alan Weaving *(Ardea);* **Page Sixteen: Middle Left,** Copyright Peter B. Kaplan 1981; **Center,** K. H. Switak; **Lower Left,** Zig Leszczynski *(Animals Animals)*; **Page Seventeen: Lower Left,** Zig Leszczynski *(Animals Animals)*; **Middle Right,** John Tashjian; **Lower Right,** Norman Owen Tomalin *(Bruce Coleman);* **Page Nineteen: Left,** Zig Lexzczynski *(Animals Animals);* **Upper Right,** K. H. Switak; **Middle Right,** Joe McDonald *(Bruce Coleman);* **Page Twenty: Upper Center,** Jean-Paul Ferrero *(Ardea);* **Right,** Tom McHugh *(Photo Researchers);* **Lower Center,** John Tashjian; **Lower Right,** John Tashjian; **Page Twenty-one Upper Left,** Zig Leszczynski *(Animals Animals);* **Center,** Ken Fink *(Ardea);* **Upper Right,** K. H. Switak; **Lower Left,** John Tashjian; **Lower Center,** John Tashjian; **Lower Right,** Kenneth Lucas; Pages **Twenty-two and Twenty-three:** Michael Fogden *(Bruce Coleman, Inc.)*.

Our Thanks To: Barbara Shattuck *(National Geographic Magazine);* Susan Hathaway *(Zoological Society of San Diego);* Michele Robinson *(San Diego Zoo Library);* Lynnette Wexo.

Creative Education would like to thank Wildlife Education, Ltd., for granting them the rights to print and distribute this hardbound edition.

Contents

Snakes are one of the world's most successful groups of animals. They live on every continent but Antarctica, and there are more than 2,700 different kinds. Most of these live on or under the ground, but some types live in trees — and some spend all or part of their lives in the water.

Secretive by nature, snakes stay away from people as much as they can. For this reason, we are not totally sure how big they can grow, or how long they can live. The longest snake ever measured was a Reticulated Python 32 feet 9½ inches (10 meters) in length. The heaviest ever weighed was an Anaconda of 600 pounds (272 kilograms). And the oldest on record was a Boa Constrictor that lived 40 years in a zoo. But, for all we know, there may be a far older and larger snake living today in one of the world's hidden places.

Shortest of snakes is the Thread Snake, a primitive and almost colorless snake that may be as little as 4¼ inches (108 millimeters) long. Most snakes are far more colorful, with a variety of colors and patterns that is truly amazing. In fact, if you can overcome the fear of snakes that most people seem to have, you will soon see that snakes are among the most beautiful creatures on earth.

FOREST COBRA
Naja melanoleuca

ROUGH-SCALED BUSH VIPER
Atheris hispidus

CALIFORNIA MOUNTAIN
KINGSNAKE
Lampropeltis zonata

GRAY-BANDED KINGSNAKE
Lampropeltis mexicana
ATTACKING
PYGMY RATTLESNAKE
Sistrurus miliarius

RETICULATED PYTHON
Python reticulatus

Peru Boa
Boa constrictor ortoni

Eastern Green Mamba
Dendroaspis angusticeps

Flying Snake
Chrysopelea paradisi

Mangrove Snake
Boiga dendrophila

Northern Copperhead
Agkistrodon contortrix mokasen

Banded Krait
Bungarus fasciatus
AND HATCHING YOUNG

Rhinoceros Viper
Bitis nasicornis

Thread Snake
Leptotyphlops bilineata

The body of a snake seems odd when you first look at it. But it has many of the same kinds of parts that the human body has—a backbone, a heart, a stomach, and so forth. These are arranged very differently, of course, but they perform the same kinds of jobs for the snake that they do for us. As with all creatures in nature, the snake has a body that is suited for the life it leads. And the sheer number of different kinds of snakes that live in the world today is proof that the design of the snake is a good one.

Unlike human beings, snakes keep growing until they die. The rate of growth is much faster when they are young, and continues to slow down as they age. An old snake may grow only a little bit . . . but it will still grow.

Many people think that snakes are "all tail," but only a part of the snake is actually a tail. In some primitive types, the tail is very short—no more than a few inches in length. And even the longest snakes rarely have a tail that is more than ⅓ the total body length.

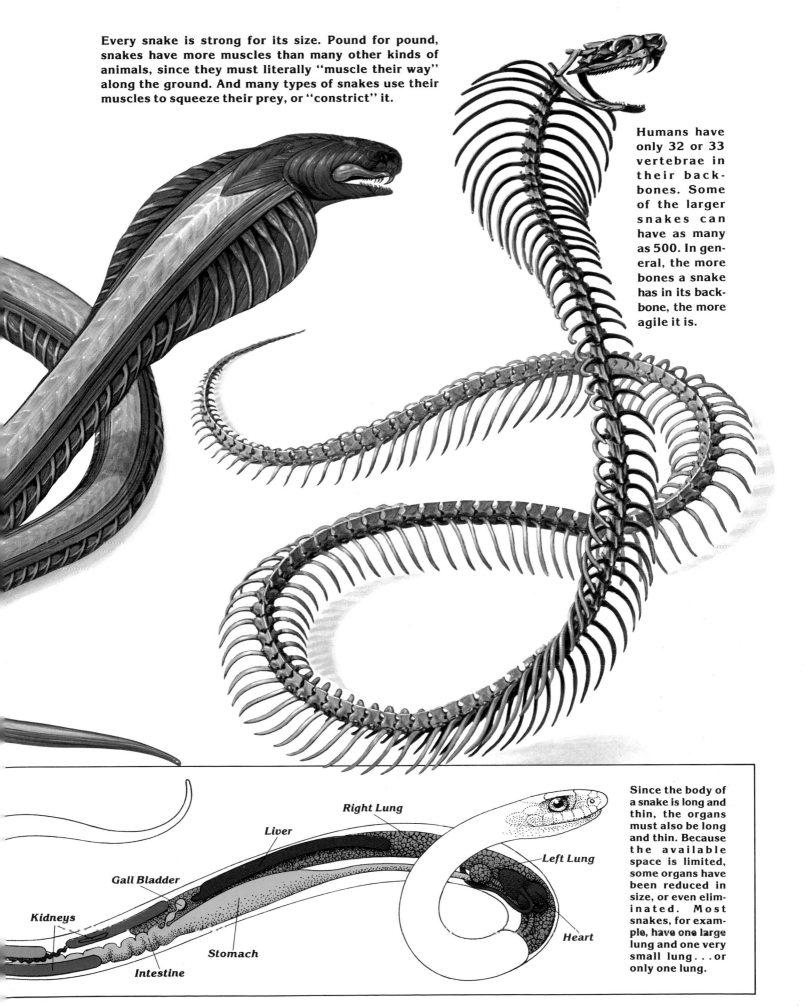

Every snake is strong for its size. Pound for pound, snakes have more muscles than many other kinds of animals, since they must literally "muscle their way" along the ground. And many types of snakes use their muscles to squeeze their prey, or "constrict" it.

Humans have only 32 or 33 vertebrae in their back-bones. Some of the larger snakes can have as many as 500. In general, the more bones a snake has in its back-bone, the more agile it is.

Right Lung

Liver

Gall Bladder

Kidneys

Stomach

Intestine

Left Lung

Heart

Since the body of a snake is long and thin, the organs must also be long and thin. Because the available space is limited, some organs have been reduced in size, or even eliminated. Most snakes, for example, have one large lung and one very small lung. . .or only one lung.

The skin of a snake is important to the survival of the animal in many ways. The hard scales protect the inside of the body from injury. The colors and patterns that are part of the skin may help to hide the snake from danger — or they may warn predators away. And, as the snake grows larger, it can shed the outer part of its skin to make room for its larger body. (A young snake that is growing rapidly may shed more than 7 times in one year.)

Snake skin has 3 layers. Only the outer, thinnest layer is peeled away when the snake sheds. The middle layer grows a new outer layer to take the place of the peeled-off layer. The scales are thickened parts of the middle and lower layers, and they are never shed. The bottom layer contains the color of the skin, which shows through the upper two layers.

Snakes are not slimy. Their skin is hard and glossy to reduce friction as the snake slides over the ground.

When a snake stretches, you can see how the scales are really "bumps" in the skin.

When a snake is ready to shed, its skin loses its shiny lustre. The eyes cloud over and the snake becomes partly blind.

Usually, the scales on a snake's head are larger than the ones on the body. Head scale patterns are unique for some species, and are sometimes used for identification.

The eyes of snakes are covered by thin transparent scales called spectacles (or brilles). These are shed along with the skin and the snake must grow new ones.

How A Snake Gets Out Of Its Skin

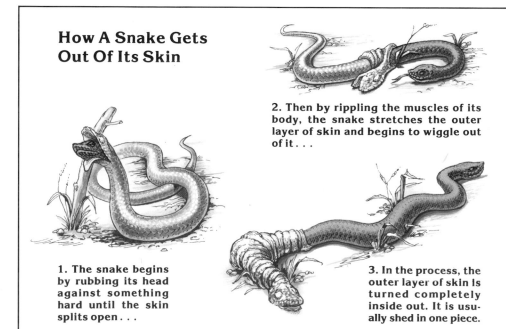

2. Then by rippling the muscles of its body, the snake stretches the outer layer of skin and begins to wiggle out of it . . .

1. The snake begins by rubbing its head against something hard until the skin splits open . . .

3. In the process, the outer layer of skin is turned completely inside out. It is usually shed in one piece.

Very poisonous
Brazilian Coral Snake
Micrurus frontalis

Mildly Poisonous
False Coral Snake
Oxyrhopus trigeminus

Scales can take strange shapes, as in the "horns" that some vipers have on their heads. These help to camouflage the outline of the snake's head and thereby help to hide it.

Sometimes, snakes may gain a great advantage by looking like other snakes, since this can protect them from predators. When a predator attacks a mildly poisonous snake, it often receives a painful bite. As a result, it learns to not attack a snake of a particular color . . . or other snakes that look similar to it. Non-poisonous and very poisonous snakes with similar patterns are therefore safer from that predator. Oddly enough, it does little good for a snake to look like a very poisonous snake, since predators that attack such snakes rarely live long enough to learn any lessons.

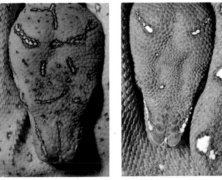

The colors of a snake may change a great deal as it grows older. At left, a very young Green Tree Python. At right, the same snake a year later.

Scales on different kinds of snakes are different shapes. Some have ridges (or "keels") running down the center.

Colors that seem very bright may actually serve to hide a snake. In the lush tropical forest, bright green can blend into the background very well.

On the underside of a snake, the scales are usually larger and thicker than those on the rest of the body. As explained on the next page, these scales are sometimes used to move the snake.

Dull colors and geometric patterns disguise the shape of a snake against certain backgrounds. Desert snakes will often increase the effectiveness of this camouflage by burying themselves in the sand.

Getting around without legs is

not as difficult as you might think. All snakes have at least three ways to move their bodies — and some have even more ways than that. Without stopping for a minute to worry about legs, snakes climb trees, swim, go almost anywhere they like. A few species in Southeast Asia even glide through the air!

Rest easy. There is no snake on earth fast enough to catch a running human being.

Scientists tell us that the ancestors of today's snakes had legs. But they took to burrowing in the ground and found that legs got in their way. Some boas and pythons—which are rather primitive types of snakes—still have small spurs on their bodies, all that is left of their ancestors' legs.

Lateral motion is the most common way of moving for all snakes. To move forward, a snake pushes *sideways* against rocks, sticks, and other objects it finds on the ground. By doing this, the snake is able to "get a grip" on the ground at several places along the length of its body.

Using the muscles attached to each of its ribs, the snake then pushes each set of ribs against each gripping point, starting with the ribs nearest its head and working back toward its tail. As each set of ribs "pushes off" in its turn, the snake moves forward.

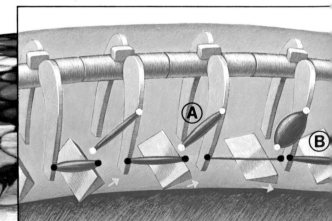

Caterpillar motion is another common method of moving, which makes use of the large belly scales ("scutes") that most snakes have. First, the muscles that attach the snake's ribs to its skin are tightened (A), pulling up the scutes and drawing them forward. Then another set of muscles (B) is tightened, and the

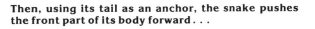

Concertina motion is used by snakes to move in tight places. First the snake bunches itself together...

Then, using its tail as an anchor, the snake pushes the front part of its body forward...

Finally, the snake anchors the front part of its body and pulls the tail forward. It is then ready to repeat the whole process all over again.

There are snakes that swim in the ocean as easily as a fish. The bodies of these sea snakes are less rounded than those of land snakes. Some of them, like the one shown at right, have paddle-shaped tails. They can swim much faster than a man.

Sidewinding makes it possible for certain snakes to "walk" across loose sand in the desert. To start this movement, the snake first arches its back and "throws" the front part of its body forward...

When the front part comes to rest on the sand, the snake loops the rest of its body forward, lifting it high above the ground...

By throwing and looping its body again and again, the snake is able to "stride" forward over the sand at a remarkably rapid rate.

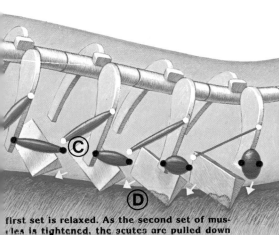

first set is relaxed. As the second set of muscles is tightened, the scutes are pulled down and back (C). They dig into the ground (D), and the snake "shovels its way" along the ground. Many sections of the snake's body repeat these motions at the same time.

Snakes are meat eaters, and they have some very effective ways to find and catch their supper. In general, snakes do not chase after their prey, but prefer to surprise it— either by sneaking up on it or by lying hidden until the unsuspecting prey comes close enough to be grabbed.

In many cases, snakes eat animals that humans consider pests, such as rats—and so the quiet efficiency of the snake as a hunter is often good for us. Even poisonous snakes do far more good for mankind than harm.

Most snakes have poor eyesight. Usually, they only see prey if it moves. They have no eyelids and cannot blink their eyes. This is why they always seem to be "staring," even when asleep.

As a group, snakes eat a wide variety of animals and insects. But there are also many animals that hunt them. Their enemies include other snakes. Below, a kingsnake attacks a rattle-snake.

The hearing of snakes is not very good, and they seldom make use of it in finding their prey. They have no outer ear, so sound must travel by way of the jawbone to reach the inner ear.

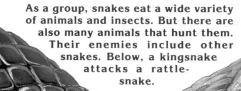

Tricks are sometimes used to attract prey. The Southern Copper-head shown above is wiggling its bright yellow tail to hold the frog's attention, while the front end of the snake gets into position to strike.

14

Constriction is used by many types of snakes to subdue their prey. The snake simply wraps itself around an animal and squeezes hard enough to keep the animal from breathing. When the animal has stopped breathing, the snake must swallow it whole, since snake teeth are not good for chewing.

The jaws of most snakes are only loosely connected to each other, so their mouths can be opened very wide. It is even possible for a snake to swallow something that is wider than its own head. After a big meal, snakes may go for a long time without eating again. One snake survived for *two years* on one meal!

Some types of snakes have very sensitive heat detectors that make it possible for them to locate their prey in the dark. Holes, or "pits," on the snake's head pick up heat given off by warm-blooded animals and tell the snake where the prey is hiding.

Some snakes live almost entirely on a diet of eggs. They are able to swallow an egg whole, and may even swallow several large eggs at a time.

Snakes do not sting with their tongues. To make up for their poor eyesight, they use their tongues to help them find out what's going on in the world around them. Flicking the tongue in and out constantly, they pick up small specks of dust from the air and ground. These are carried into the mouth and placed in taste detectors called Jacobson's Organs. The taste of the specks tells the snake what animals are near, and other things as well.

Inside the throat of an egg-eating snake, there are a series of sharp bones that cut eggs open as they are swallowed. The contents of the egg continue on down the throat, while the crushed eggshell is pushed back out of the mouth.

Many snakes can swallow animals that are almost as big as they are . . . and this means that the largest snakes can probably swallow incredibly large things. Record books tell us of an African Rock Python, weighing no more than 140 pounds (63½ kilograms) that swallowed an animal that weighed more than 130 pounds (59 kilograms).

Poisonous snakes use venom because it is a very good way to capture prey. There is no need for a poisonous snake to spend hours and a great deal of energy squeezing its prey, and there is no need to chase after prey. The snake simply injects its venom and waits for it to take effect.

Of the 2,700 different kinds of snakes in the world, only about 400 are poisonous to some degree. Of these, fewer than 50 are really dangerous to man. The rest are either too timid to attack people or they do not inject enough venom to do much harm. Some of the snakes that are most dangerous to people are shown on these pages.

Rear-fanged snakes, such as the African Boomslang below, have rather small fangs. These are so far back in the mouth that the snake must really get its mouth around something before the fangs can do their job. The fangs are U-shaped (as shown), and instead of injecting venom they merely channel it.

The largest of all venomous snakes is the King Cobra. It sometimes grows to a length of over 18 feet (5½ meters).

Black Mambas are probably the most dangerous snakes in Africa. These long and thin snakes can move very fast, and can inject enough venom to kill 10 men.

The venom of Saw-scaled Vipers is particularly toxic to man. Even when it is only 10 inches (25 centimeters) long, this snake has enough venom to kill.

Front-fanged snakes, including the Coral Snake shown at right, have fangs in a better position to deliver a dose of venom than those of rear-fanged snakes. The fangs are still rather small, but they are rounded enough to inject the venom more efficiently.

Large-fanged snakes, like the Timber Rattlesnake shown at left, are able to inject venom very efficiently. The fangs fold up when the mouth is closed, but can swing into position to strike the moment the mouth is opened. Each fang is long and hollow like a hypodermic needle, so venom can be injected under pressure.

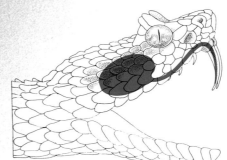

Many vipers have venom glands so large that the sides of their heads are expanded to make room for them. A heart-shaped head is a sure way to identify these poisonous snakes, since no other snakes have heads of a similar shape.

Australia's Tiger Snake is one of the most poisonous snakes on a continent that has many deadly snakes. Four out of every ten people it bites do not survive.

The Western Diamondback Rattlesnake is probably the most dangerous snake in North America. It has a very short temper and can inject enough venom at one time to kill 45 people.

Gaboon Vipers have the largest fangs of any poisonous snake—as much as 2 inches (51 millimeters) in length, and very sharp.

Snakes don't want to poison you. Their venom is intended for catching prey, and they would rather not waste it on an animal (you) that they cannot eat. In most parts of the world you can avoid being bitten by a poisonous snake if you will take just a few simple precautions.

As the map at right shows, the highest fatalities from snakebite occur in areas where many varieties of poisonous snakes live close to places where people live, and where medical care is often not available. In India and Burma, which both have many kinds of venomous snakes, more than 18,000 people die each year from snakebite.

DANGER OF SNAKEBITE

☐ None
Extremely Small
Very Very Small
Very Small
Small
Moderate
Above Average

In the United States, only 15 people are killed each year by snakes (while more than 140 are killed *every day* in highway accidents). There are places where the death rate is much higher, but snakebite is not really a major cause of death anywhere. Worldwide, only 1 out of every 115,000 people will be killed each year by snakebite.

To Avoid Being Bitten By A Snake...

DO prepare yourself before going into areas where poisonous snakes live. Read about the kinds of snakes you may find, so you will be able to recognize dangerous snakes when you see them.

DO NOT go into snake country unless you are properly dressed. Wear heavy leather high-top boots and loose-fitting pants, and let the cuffs of the pants hang outside the boots.

DO NOT make sudden moves if you see a poisonous snake or hear a rattling sound. Snakes cannot see you as well if you don't move too much. Be careful you don't back away from one snake and run into another nearby.

DO NOT sleep on the ground. You may roll over on a snake while asleep—or a snake may crawl in next to you to get warm!

DO NOT reach or step into places before you can see clearly if snakes are hiding there. Never reach over your head while climbing, unless you can see where your hand is going, and *look* over logs before you *step* over them.

If You Are Bitten...

DO NOT PANIC! Be sure the snake has actually sunk its fangs into you and be sure it is a poisonous snake. Many times, snakes will not use their fangs or will not inject poison—and many people have been "poisoned" by perfectly harmless snakes. DO NOT try to catch the snake, because it may bite you again . . . but DO try to get a good look at it.

DO NOT try to treat the wound yourself, unless it is absolutely impossible to get to a doctor quickly. Many people do more damage to themselves trying to treat a snakebite than the snake has done.

DO get to a doctor as quickly as you can, but DO NOT run. Physical exertion causes the heart to pump blood faster, and will make the poison spread faster.

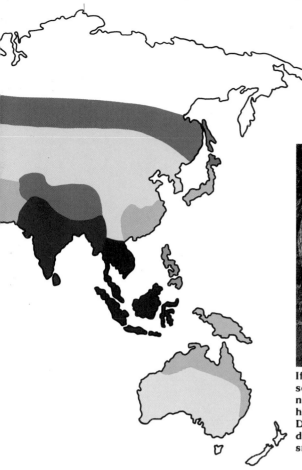

Snakes do a variety of things when they try to scare an intruder away. Most of them hiss loudly, and many—like the African Boomslang at right—will swell up their necks, attempting to look larger and more dangerous.

When a snake shows you the inside of its mouth, and the lining is brightly colored, move away. The snake is very likely to be poisonous.

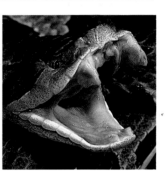

If an intruder does not scare easily, some types of snakes—like this hognose snake—will "play dead" and hope that the intruder will go away. Do not touch a snake that looks dead, since even a non-poisonous snake can give you a nasty bite.

The only use that a rattlesnake has for its rattle is to scare away animals it does not want to kill. When it is hunting, the rattle remains silent, so that the prey will not be warned of the rattler's approach. The sound of a rattle can often be heard up to 60 feet away.

When a person and a snake meet, the snake will usually do everything it can to get away, or to scare the person away. Only when the snake is surprised by the sudden appearance of an intruder, or when it cannot get away, will it usually bite.

19

Behavior of snakes is influenced to a great extent by the weather. Like other reptiles, they are cold-blooded — the temperature of their bodies depends on the temperature of the air. As a result, air temperature determines where snakes can live, when they will be active, when they will mate, and other things as well. In general, snakes are most comfortable in temperatures between 70° Fahrenheit (21° Celsius) and 99° Fahrenheit (37° Celsius). If the temperature falls below 39°F (4°C), or rises above 100°F (38°C), most snakes will die.

When the air is chilly, snakes often lie in the sun. By basking in this way, they can raise their body temperatures above the temperature of the surrounding air. In hot weather, snakes will often bury themselves in the sand, or hide under a bush or a rock, to lower their body temperatures.

Finding a place to keep warm when the weather gets cold can be a life-and-death matter for a snake. Many snakes "hole up" for the winter in caves. During the rest of the year, snakes usually live alone, but when they shelter for the winter many species share their dens with other snakes of their own kind. Sometimes, hundreds of snakes will occupy the same den.

As the weather above ground gets colder, the snakes in the den hibernate. They become lethargic and may even appear to be dead. When warm weather returns, however, they revive and leave the den in search of food. Spring is also the time when most snakes go looking for mates.

Scientific experiments show that there is a wide range of variation in the temperatures that snakes from different climates prefer. Snakes from colder climates feel most comfortable in temperatures that are a full 15° Fahrenheit (9.4° Celsius) cooler than temperatures preferred by snakes from desert climates.

Colder Climate
ALPINE VIPER

Temperate Climate
EASTERN HOGNOSE SNAKE

Some snakes give birth to live young. The mother carries egg sacks containing the babies inside her until the young are ready to be born. Then she pushes the sacks out of her body and the babies break out of them. With some species, as many as 80 live young may be born at the same time.

Sometimes, snakes are born with two heads. Each head behaves like a separate snake, and heads will sometimes even nip at each other or fight over food.

Most snakes lay eggs, from which the young hatch later. To protect the babies inside them, the eggs are tough and leathery, and the young snakes sometimes have a difficult time breaking out of them. They have special egg teeth to help them cut through the shell.

Combat "dances" are performed by some types of male snakes in the Spring. They rear up, twist around, and try to scare each other—but nobody usually gets hurt.

Female snakes leave scent trails to help males find them. When mating, the two snakes may wrap their tails together.

Sub-tropical climate
COTTONMOUTH

Tropical Forest Climate
MALAYSIAN SHORT PYTHON

Desert Climate
MEXICAN GRAY-BANDED KINGSNAKE

Index